rockschool®

Drums Grade 6

*Performance pieces, technical exercises and in-depth guidance
for Rockschool examinations*

www.rockschool.co.uk

Acknowledgements

Published by Rockschool Ltd. © 2012
Catalogue Number RSK051225
ISBN: 978-1-908920-24-9
Revision 1 | 8 February 2013 | Errata details can be found at *www.rockschool.co.uk*

AUDIO
Recorded at Fisher Lane Studios
Produced and engineered by Nick Davis
Assistant engineer and Pro Tools operator Mark Binge
Mixed and mastered at Langlei Studios
Mixing and additional editing by Duncan Jordan
Supporting Tests recorded by Duncan Jordan and Kit Morgan
Mastered by Duncan Jordan
Executive producers James Uings, Jeremy Ward and Noam Lederman

MUSICIANS
James Arben, Joe Bennett, Jason Bowld, Larry Carlton, Stuart Clayton, Andy Crompton, Neel Dhorajiwala, Fergus Gerrand, Charlie Griffiths, Felipe Karam, Kishon Khan, Noam Lederman, DJ Harry Love, Dave Marks, Kit Morgan, Jon Musgrave, Jake Painter, Richard Pardy, Ross Stanley, Stuart Ryan, Carl Sterling, Henry Thomas, Camilo Tirado, Simon Troup, James Uings, Steve Walker, Chris Webster, Norton York, Nir Z

PUBLISHING
Fact Files written by Luke Aldridge, Jason Bowld, Neel Dhorajiwala, Stephen Lawson, Noam Lederman and David West
Walkthroughs written by Noam Lederman
Music engraving and book layout by Simon Troup and Jennie Troup of Digital Music Art
Proof and copy editing by Noam Lederman, Claire Davies, Stephen Lawson, Simon Pitt and James Uings
Publishing administration by Caroline Uings
Cover design by Philip Millard

SYLLABUS
Syllabus director: Jeremy Ward
Instrumental specialists: Stuart Clayton, Noam Lederman and James Uings
Special thanks to: Brad Fuller and Georg Voros

SPONSORSHIP
Noam Lederman plays Mapex Drums, PAISTE cymbals and uses Vic Firth Sticks
Nir Z plays GMS drums, Sabian cymbals, PRO-MARK drumsticks, Evans drumheads, Gibraltar hardware
Rockschool would like to thank the following companies for donating instruments used in the cover artwork

PRINTING
Printed and bound in the United Kingdom by Caligraving Ltd
CDs manufactured in the European Union by Software Logistics

DISTRIBUTION
Exclusive Distributors: Music Sales Ltd

CONTACTING ROCKSCHOOL
www.rockschool.co.uk
Telephone: +44 (0)845 460 4747
Fax: +44 (0)845 460 1960

Table of Contents

Introductions & Information

Rockschool Grade Pieces

Technical Exercises

Supporting Tests

Additional Information

Welcome to Rockschool Drums Grade 6

Welcome to Drums Grade 6

Welcome to the Rockschool Drums Grade 6 pack. This book and CD contain everything you need to play drums at this grade. In the book you will find the exam scores in drum notation. The CD has full stereo mixes of each tune, backing tracks to play along to for practice and spoken two bar count-ins to both the full mixes and backing track versions of the songs. There are two backing tracks of each song: one with a click and one without. You can choose which one to play along with in the exam.

Drum Exams

At each grade, you have the option of taking one of two different types of examination:

- **Grade Exam:** a Grade Exam is a mixture of music performances, technical work and tests. You prepare three pieces (two of which may be Free Choice Pieces) and the contents of the Technical Exercise section. This accounts for 75% of the exam marks. The other 25% consists of a Quick Study Piece (10%), a pair of instrument specific Ear Tests (10%), and finally you will be asked five General Musicianship Questions (5%). The pass mark is 60%.

- **Performance Certificate:** in a Performance Certificate you play five pieces. Up to three of these can be Free Choice Pieces. Each song is marked out of 20 and the pass mark is 60%.

Book Contents

The book is divided into a number of sections. These are:

- **Exam Pieces:** in this book you will find six specially commissioned pieces of Grade 6 standard. Each of these is preceded by a *Fact File*. Each Fact File contains a summary of the song, its style, tempo, key and technical features, along with a list of the musicians who played on it. There is additional information on the techniques and style as well as recommended further listening. The song itself is printed on up to four pages. Immediately after each song is a *Walkthrough*. This covers the song from a performance perspective, focusing on the technical issues you will encounter. Each Walkthrough features two graphical musical 'highlights' showing particular parts of the song. Each song comes with a full mix version and a backing track. Both versions have spoken count-ins at the beginning. Please note that any solos played on the full mix versions are indicative only.

- **Technical Exercises:** you should prepare the exercises set in this grade in the keys indicated. You should also choose *one* Stylistic Study from the three printed to practise and play to the backing track in the exam. The style you choose will determine the style of the Quick Study Piece.

- **Supporting Tests and General Musicianship Questions:** in Drums Grade 6 there are three supporting tests – a Quick Study Piece, a pair of Ear Tests and a set of General Musicianship Questions (GMQs) asked at the end of each exam. Examples of the types of tests likely to appear in the exam are printed in this book. Additional test examples of both types of test and the GMQs can be found in the Rockschool *Companion Guide to Drums*.

- **Grade 7 Preview:** we have included in this book one of the songs found in the Grade 7 Drums book as a taster. The piece is printed with its Fact File and Walkthrough, and the full mix and backing tracks can be found on the CD.

- **General Information:** finally, you will find information on exam procedures, including online examination entry, marking schemes, and what to do when arriving, and waiting, for your exam.

We hope you enjoy using this book. You will find a *Syllabus Guide* for Drums and other exam information on our website: *www.rockschool.co.uk*. Rockschool Graded Music Exams are accredited in England, Wales and Northern Ireland by Ofqual, the DfE and CCEA and by SQA Accreditation in Scotland.

SONG TITLE: MOHAIR MOUNTAIN
GENRE: CLASSIC ROCK
TEMPO: 92 BPM

TECH FEATURES: ODD TIME SIGNATURES
TEMPO CHANGES
BASS DRUM DOUBLES

COMPOSERS: JOE BENNETT
& KUNG FU DRUMMER

PERSONNEL: NOAM LEDERMAN (DRUMS)
STUART RYAN (GTR)
HENRY THOMAS (BASS)

OVERVIEW

'Mohair Mountain' is a classic rock track written in the style of bands such as Led Zeppelin and Deep Purple, and based on the drumming of John Bonham and Ian Paice. The track features time changes and a shift in feel from straight to swung, a common feature of this style.

STYLE FOCUS

Classic rock drummers must have an array of skills to hand. Being able to play swung or straight and to switch note values seamlessly when filling are some of the most important attributes of a drummer. Feel is also important because the music often conveys a range of emotions and dynamics which need to be complemented convincingly by the drum kit. Your leading bass drum foot must be up to speed to accurately perform those 16th triplet bursts in the spirit of Led Zeppelin's John Bonham.

THE BIGGER PICTURE

The term classic rock is usually applied to guitar bands from the 1970s and 1980s. However, the genre has it roots in the late 1960s when bands like Cream

and The Who were pushing amplifiers to their limits and recording extended tracks far beyond the remit of the 45 rpm single.

In the 1970s Led Zeppelin and Deep Purple dominated this style of music, although Led Zeppelin's recording career was curtailed in 1980 by the death of their drummer John Bonham. Bonham was one of the most influential rock drummers of all time and had many attributes that most drummers can only dream of: incredible power, a fast bass drum foot and ferocious hand speed coupled with a unique feel for the groove of a song. Led Zeppelin reunited in 2007 with John Bonham's son Jason continuing his father's legacy in the drum stool.

RECOMMENDED LISTENING

Researching this style of music will give you great pleasure as a drummer for the standard of musicianship is incredibly high. Ginger Baker's work with Cream on *Fresh Cream* demonstrates creativity in its fills and grooves, particularly on the track 'Toad' which features an excellent melodic drum solo. Led Zeppelin's 'Good Times Bad Times' stands out for its fast bass drum work and dynamic fills; 'Moby Dick', for its characteristic grooving; and 'Fool in the Rain', for that classic Bonham shuffle.

Mohair Mountain

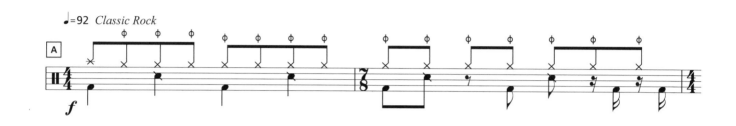

Joe Bennett & Kung Fu Drummer

♩=92 *Classic Rock*

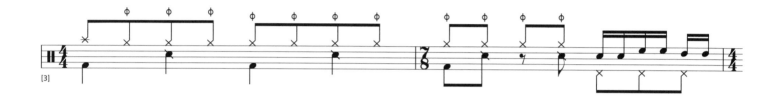

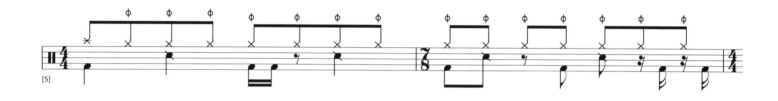

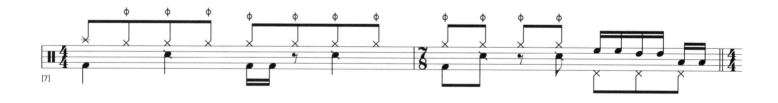

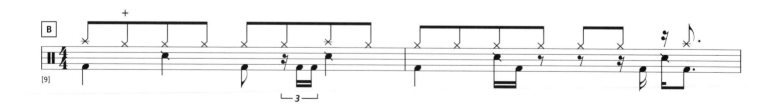

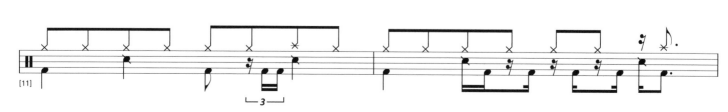

This music is copyright. Photocopying is illegal.

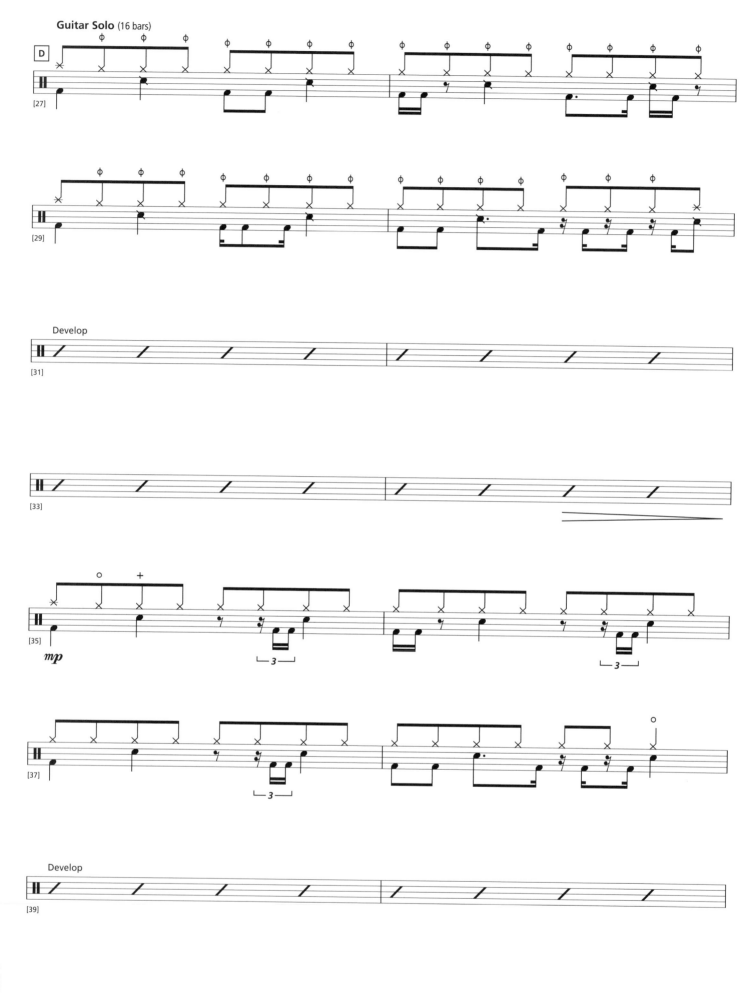

Walkthrough

A Section (Bars 1–8)
This section features the intro riff of the song which consists of alternating 4/4 and 7/8 bars. The heavy rock groove is built from half open hi-hats, rim-shot snare on the backbeat and a bass drum figure that is typical of the genre.

Bar 1 | *Half open hi-hat*
The vertical line through the open hi-hat mark indicates that the hi-hat should be only half open in this section. This can be done by tightening your foot on the hi-hat pedal. Ideally, the hi-hat cymbals will be consistently close to each other and produce a sizzling sound.

Bars 1–8 | *Changing time signatures*
In this section the time signature alternates from four quarter notes to seven eighth notes in a bar. Listen to the guitar and bass riff carefully in order to understand the phrasing. If you are using the backing track with the click, you will hear it changing from quarter notes to eighth notes in order to help you follow. At this level, you should be able to move smoothly between time signatures without affecting the flow of time.

B Section (Bars 9–16)
This is the verse part of the song and the hi-hat should mostly stay closed. The challenging foot work with the bass drum is typical of this genre and will require solid technique.

Bar 9 | *Fast bass drums*
Playing the two consecutive 16th triplet notes at this speed will demand preparation. Slowing the tempo down and breaking down the groove is a good way to start practising. Although this can be played with both heel up and heel down techniques, you might want to attempt a unique sliding motion with your bass drum foot. Place your bass drum foot in the heel up position and pull your foot back until your toes are in the middle of the footplate. Perform the first stroke and allow the beater to continue its natural movement in order to create a second stroke as a rebound of the first. When played correctly, this technique will allow you to perform two strokes with one movement. The concept is similar to performing doubles with your hands and the same rules apply: practise slowly and internalise the movement (Fig. 1).

C Section (Bars 17–26)
In this section you will return to the half open hi-hat with a busier bass drum pattern and drags on the snare.

Bar 17 | *Drag*
The drag rudiment consists of two grace notes followed by one main stroke. In this groove, the drag is played on the snare and the main stroke on the bass drum and hi-hat.

Ensure that you control the stick to achieve two even grace notes and time these well in between the eight-note hi-hats.

D Section (Bars 27–42)
The D section consists of a 16-bar guitar solo. It comprises two grooves with slightly different feels and bars that need to be developed stylistically. Make sure that you observe the changes in dynamics in bars 35 and 42.

E Section (Bars 43–50)
The eight bar drum solo is based on the structure of the intro, where the time signature changes. Listen to John Bonham (Led Zeppelin) for ideas for solos in this style.

F Section (Bars 51–69)
The tempo changes from 92 bpm to 126 bpm in bar 51 and the groove moves to the ride cymbal. There are rim-shots and ghost notes to consider as well as stylistic fills with advanced hand-foot coordination.

Bar 67 | *3:2 polyrhythm*
In this fill you have to co-ordinate quarter-note triplets with quarter notes. That means that every two beats, a full quarter-note triplet will be played, hence '3:2 polyrhythm'. Use your hi-hat foot as your anchor and focus on performing the triplets accurately with conviction (Fig. 2).

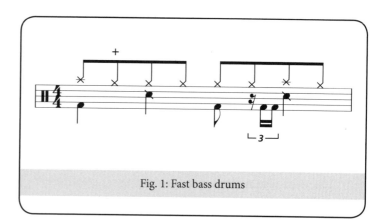

Fig. 1: Fast bass drums

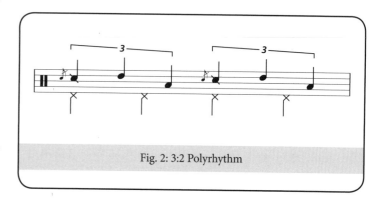

Fig. 2: 3:2 Polyrhythm

Pop It In The ToP

Pop It In The ToP

SONG TITLE: POP IT IN THE TOP
GENRE: FUNK
TEMPO: 110 BPM

TECH FEATURES: SNARE GHOSTING
                 LINEAR FUNK BEATS
                 DOUBLES

COMPOSER: LUKE ALDRIDGE

PERSONNEL: STUART RYAN (GTR)
               HENRY THOMAS (BASS)
               NIR Z (DRUMS)
               FULL FAT HORNS (BRASS)
               ROSS STANLEY (KEYS)
               FERGUS GERRAND (PERC)

OVERVIEW

'Pop It In The ToP' is a funk track written in the style of American R&B band Tower Of Power. It features snare ghosting, linear funk beats and doubles.

STYLE FOCUS

Within this piece there are a variety of different grooves that reflect elements of Tower Of Power drummer David Garibaldi's playing and those of other drummers who have played with the group over the years. The piece starts with a simple beat that throws in some 16ths and eighths between the hands in the second bar, an idea that is revisited later in the piece. There are also more 'linear' grooves that use different sticking and hand and foot combinations rather than a constant eighth- or 16th-note hi-hat pattern. Although these are more challenging to play, it is essential that they flow well and sit just as comfortably as the less complicated beats do.

THE BIGGER PICTURE

The roots of Tower Of Power go back to 1968 when, influenced by James Brown, they established a funk based style that was distinctly their own. Formed by tenor saxophonist and vocalist Emilio Castillo and baritone saxophonist Stephen Kupka, the band's hard hitting funk grooves mixed with lush R&B chord progressions and soul tinged vocals proved popular with funk and soul fans.

The band's instrumental line-up has remained the same despite personnel changes: a signature horn section (two trumpets, two tenor saxes and a baritone sax), vocals, guitar, keyboards, bass and drums.

Tower Of Power's instantly recognisable sound is largely due to its linear drum style combined with staccato, syncopated horn riffs and busy basslines.

RECOMMENDED LISTENING

Tower Of Power have recorded 18 studio albums but a good place to start is their live offering *Soul Vaccination: Live* (1999), which featured the return of original drummer Garibaldi. *Souled Out* (1995), with Herman Riley on drums, includes the great 'Soul With A Capital S' and 'Diggin' On James Brown'. 'Drop it In The Slot', from the album *In the Slot* (1975), is an obvious influence on 'Pop It In The ToP' and is played by the band's classic line-up, as does the album *Live And In Living Color* (1976), which is a rare live recording from their late 1970s period.

11

Pop It In The ToP

Luke Aldridge

12

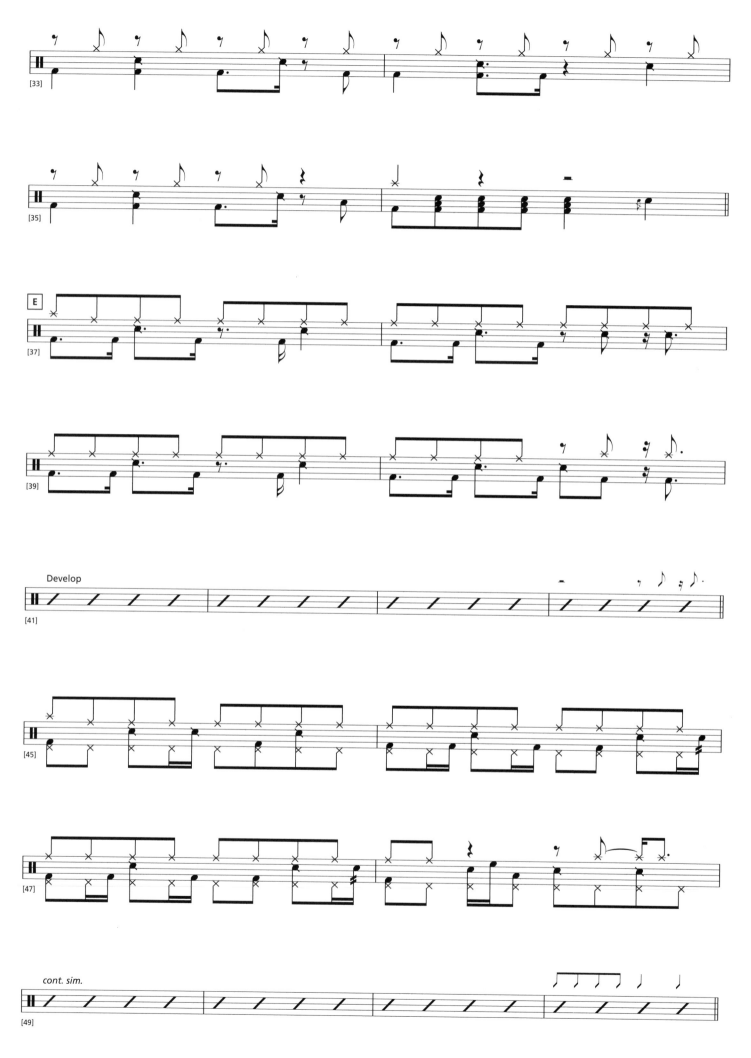

Walkthrough

A Section (Bars 1–4)
This is a drum introduction that establishes the main funk groove. There are 16th-note bass drums, rim-shot snares and a fill in bar 4.

B Section (Bars 5–20)
This is the verse part of the song where the groove remains similar to the intro. There are stylistic fills and snare/bass drum variations.

Bar 6 | *Alternating 16th*
On the second beat of this bar there are four 16th notes that alternate between the snare and the hi-hat. Keep your left hand on the snare in order to execute the rim-shot snares and co-ordinate the hi-hats accurately in between. Make sure that the flow of the groove is not affected by this linear funk approach.

Bar 16 | *Sextuplet fill*
There is a sextuplet that uses the high tom and snare on the fourth beat of this bar. This fast phrase can be played with various sticking options. Try using the inverted paradiddle-diddle sticking (R L L R R L) because this will help you to achieve a natural flow. Also, aim to keep all the strokes even and accurate.

Bar 20 | *Thirty-second notes*
There are 32nd notes to perform in this fill. These are the next subdivision after 16th notes, so eight of them put together are equal to one quarter note. In order to understand the rhythm on beat three, start by playing four 16th notes on the snare then double the first and create two 32nd notes. This can be played with singles: RL R L R. When replacing the last stroke with the bass drum the sticking will be as follows: RL R L F. The alternative is to use doubles at the beginning of the phrase: RR L R L or LL R L R. However, you will require reliable sticking control in order to perform these with appropriate projection (Fig. 1).

C Section (Bars 21–28)
The second main groove is introduced in the C section. This is in the form of a linear pattern with consistent 16th notes on the hi-hat and snare. It is vital that the rim-shot and ghost note snares are clear, balanced and projected well.

Bar 21 | *Ghost notes*
The snare notes marked in brackets should be played as ghost notes. The dynamic level of the ghost notes should be much lower than the non-ghosted snare strokes. Keep your hand close to the drum head in order to produce this sound naturally and hit the middle of the drum for the most rounded tone (Fig. 2).

D Section (Bars 29–36)
The breakdown section has an offbeat eighth-note hi-hat groove that develops over the course of these eight bars. Ensure that every bass drum and snare stroke are performed with conviction.

E Section (Bars 37–52)
The groove moves to the ride cymbal in this section and there is room for you to develop the part. From bar 45 a consistent eighth-note hi-hat foot pattern is added as well as syncopated crashes.

F Section (Bars 53–60)
This solo can be interpreted in various ways besides the stabs in bar 58. Whether you decide to base your solo on the rhythmic phrase played on the track or not, you must ensure that the solo is in keeping with the genre, that it develops throughout and is performed confidently. Listening to the drummer David Garibaldi (Tower of Power) will give you ideas for improvising in this style.

G (Bars 61–68) & H Section (Bars 69–76)
Section G is a reprise of the chorus with the linear funk groove. Section H is a reprise of the verse which leads to the ending phrase in bar 76.

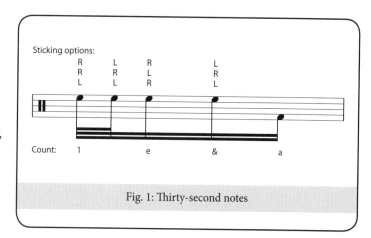

Fig. 1: Thirty-second notes

Fig. 2: Ghost notes

SONG TITLE: MINDSWEEPER

GENRE: DRUM AND BASS/METAL

TEMPO: 164 BPM

TECH FEATURES: ACCENTED ROLLS

GHOSTING

POLYRHYTHMS

COMPOSER: JASON BOWLD

PERSONNEL: JASON BOWLD (ALL PARTS)

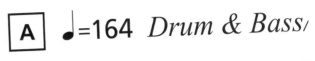

OVERVIEW

'Mindsweeper' is a typical drum and bass/metal crossover influenced by drummers such as Paul Kodish and Incubus' Jose Pasillas as well as bands like Pendulum and Pitchshifter. The song features a variety of typical drum and bass grooves that integrate ghost notes and accented rolls further embellished with broken ride cymbal patterns.

STYLE FOCUS

Drum and bass typically features a strong bass drum pattern played on the '1' and '3 &' while retaining a heavy backbeat on the snare. The ghost notes played between these pulses set up the style's distinctive feel. So, accurate dynamics are crucial: make sure your backbeats are louder than your ghost notes. This is also important when executing the various rolls in the track because they have specific accents that give them their groove-like shape.

THE BIGGER PICTURE

During the 1990s, drum and bass grew around the London and Bristol club scenes. The classic drum and bass beats (or breaks) were sampled from vinyl records (the most popular being 'Amen, Brother' by The Winstons) then sped up using software for an electronic feel. DJs Goldie and Roni Size were pioneers of this approach.

Drummers caught onto this style and started to replicate these sampled beats. They infused metal and rock with drum and bass rhythms, sometimes creating new styles such as industrial.

Pitchshifter were one of the first bands to produce this hybrid sound by using a mixture of live drums and sampled electronic sounds. Incubus also used drum and bass elements to complement their melodic sound, which sat perfectly with the funky style of drummer Pasillas.

Another notable band is Pendulum, who have been successful with a more commercial style that combines drum and bass with rock.

RECOMMENDED LISTENING

Incubus' 'Pardon Me' contains great live drum and bass breaks. For a more electronic sound listen to 'Tarantula' by Pendulum. Finally, Pitchshifter's album *www.pitchshifter.com* (1998) features some classic drum and bass breaks on 'Please Sir' and 'Genius'.

Mindsweeper

Jason Bowld

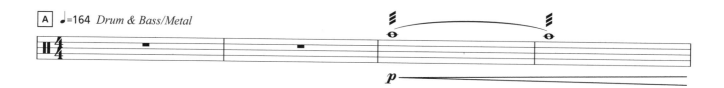

20

Walkthrough

A Section (Bars 1–16)

The intro to 'Mindsweeper' starts with a cymbal swell that leads into an abstract drum and bass groove then progresses to contemporary drum and bass grooving. It ends with an accented snare roll.

Bars 2–4 | *Cymbal roll*

This cymbal roll must start quietly and increase gradually in volume over two bars to be effective. The main tip is not to get too loud too soon.

Bars 9–14 | *Drum and bass groove on the ride*

This groove is characterised mainly by the ghost notes and bass drums played on the "1" and "3 &". Dynamics are key in sounding convincing here so make sure the backbeats are noticeably louder than the ghost notes.

Bars 15–16 | *Accented snare roll*

This is the feature roll of the song and you will need to be aware of the offbeat accents that precede the accents on the beat to make this sound correct.

B Section (Bars 17–22)

In this section the groove is intensified by extra crashes. The accented snare roll continues throughout this section.

Bars 17–20 | *Cymbal accents*

The groove played in these bars is almost identical to the previous one, except that crashes are played on beat four of every bar.

C Section (Bars 23–32)

The contemporary drum and bass groove continues in this section then progresses on to the ride for a broken pattern. The section concludes with a powerful snare roll.

Bars 23–27 | *Hi-hat embellishments*

In this drum and bass groove section, your left hand alternates between playing the ghost notes on the snare and moving to the hi-hat to create an embellishment in every other bar. For this try using the same sticking, which from beat two of bar 24 would be R/L . R L R L . L . R L. Watch out for the displaced backbeat on the "3 &" of bar 27 (Fig. 1).

Bars 28–32 | *Broken ride groove*

The broken ride pattern here is two bars long and has a dotted quarter-note feel. It is important that you play accurately from the ride surface to the bell to get the right sound. You will need to practise this groove slowly in isolation before building up to speed to deal with its complexity. The counting would be "1 2& &4 1& 2& 3& 4" during bars 28 and 29 (Fig. 2).

D Section (Bars 33–53)

This section features what could be called the chorus followed by a reprise of section B but with a different groove.

Bars 37–40 | *Chorus groove half-time*

You will need to focus on the click here because the quarter note, half-time feel will reveal any timing discrepancies.

E Section (Bars 54–69)

In this section the dynamics drop to a cross-stick groove that develops and builds into a crescendo.

Bars 54–67 | *Cross-stick development*

Consistency on the hi-hat is vital here to retain the dynamic. Small wrist movements will help, as will finding the part of the stick which produces the sweetest cross-stick sound. Increasing the bass drum frequency and adding open hi-hats would be a good way to develop this groove further.

F Section (Bars 70–86)

This is a reprise of the chorus grooves from the D section and features improvised fills.

Bars 70–81 | *Fill development*

Following the dotted quarter note crash bars, you have a chance to shine with your own fills. Try using a variety of note values and pitches to create interest.

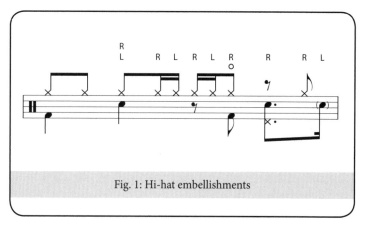

Fig. 1: Hi-hat embellishments

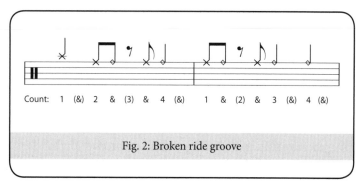

Fig. 2: Broken ride groove

SONG TITLE: FAVELA

GENRE: SAMBA

TEMPO: 109 BPM

TECH FEATURES: FOUR-WAY CO-ORDINATION
SYNCOPATED GROOVES

COMPOSER: NOAM LEDERMAN

PERSONNEL: NOAM LEDERMAN (DRUMS)
HENRY THOMAS (BASS)
STUART RYAN (GTR)
KISHON KHAN (KEYS)
FERGUS GERRAND (PERC)
RICHARD PARDY (SAX)
STEVE WALKER (TRUMPET)
ANDY CROMPTON (TROMB)

OVERVIEW

'Favela' is written in the style of Brazilian samba and features four-way co-ordination, syncopated grooves and syncopated fills among its techniques.

STYLE FOCUS

Traditionally, the samba beat was created by a group of percussionists playing different patterns. From the 1960s these patterns were adapted for the drum kit, placing each pattern on a different drum or cymbal voice. This is the reason why samba and, indeed, most Latin beats involve advanced co-ordination, making them particularly attractive to drummers of all levels.

THE BIGGER PICTURE

Samba is the rhythmic, syncopated music of Brazil with its roots in the country's African culture. The first samba record is believed to be 'Pelo Telefone', released in 1917. It gave the style its first significant exposure outside of the *favelas* (slums). It made such an impression that, in the 1930s, the nationalist dictatorship in power supported its promotion to the national music of Brazil. Early samba relied on drums and percussion (think of the sound of Rio De Janeiro's carnival marching bands) and was revered for its raw energy rather than musical sophistication. However, this changed in the 1950s when João Gilberto and Antonio Carlos Jobim brought in supple melodies and jazz influenced harmonies. This new style or 'bossa nova' exposed Brazilian music to the world. Its best-known song is 'The Girl From Ipanema', which was translated from Portuguese into English and performed by Frank Sinatra.

Bossa nova's sense of sophistication and restraint made it ideal for hotel lounges and Las Vegas theatres, but new left-wing politics were afoot in Brazil in the late 1960s. The sounds and sentiment of the *favelas* erupted through the music of Chico Buarque, Caetano Veloso and Os Mutantes, a molten fusion of samba, rock, funk and jazz. Its name was tropicalia and it remains popular to this day.

RECOMMENDED LISTENING

Gilberto's *Chega de Saudade* (1959) is a classic bossa nova record. To hear how Brazilian music changed in the 1960s, listen to the albums *Caetano Veloso* (1969) and Buarque's *Construção* (1971).

Favela

Noam Lederman

Drums Grade 6

© Copyright 2012 Rock School Ltd.

Walkthrough

A Section (Bars 1–8)
The main samba groove is introduced in the first four bars of this piece. You will require all of your limbs to perform this groove. From bar 5 there are rhythmic stabs to perform. They must be synchronised with the track.

Bar 1 | *Samba*
This is one of the traditional and basic ways of playing samba on the drum kit. Start by playing the feet pattern and work on your accuracy and flow. The bass drum can be played with the heel up technique, but you will achieve the right sound more naturally if you use heel down. Ensure that you can play this pattern comfortably and that your posture remains balanced before adding the hand pattern. The consistent eighth notes on the ride should not be too challenging to co-ordinate. However, you will need to pay attention when you add the syncopated accented snares.

Bar 4 | *Latin rim-shot*
A Latin rim-shot is produced by hitting the snare and surrounding rim at the same time with the neck part of your drum stick. This will produce a higher pitch and slightly softer rim-shot sound than the rock equivalent. Performing this technique in a relaxed way will help you to achieve the stylistic conviction that is required at this level.

B Section (Bars 9–16)
This is the verse part of the song where the groove remains similar to the intro. There is a stylistic fill using your hands and feet in bar 12, followed by a preparation fill in bar 16. This fill leads to the C section.

Bar 16 | *Syncopated fill*
The open hi-hats and crash emphasise the 'a' and 'e' and create a feeling of syncopation. Ensure that all open/closed hi-hats are projected well and that the rhythms are performed accurately (Fig. 1).

C Section (Bars 17–24)
In the chorus section a samba funk groove is introduced. Both hands play 16th notes on the hi-hat. Your right hand will move to the snare on the backbeat. The bass drum pattern maintains the traditional samba feel in this groove.

Bar 18 | *Samba funk*
The bass drum in samba funk maintains the dotted 16th-note pattern on every beat. Aim to play the bass drum strokes evenly and maintain a balanced posture. Your hands play alternate sticking on the hi-hat with offbeat accents. You will be able to perform the accent correctly by lifting your hand higher or striking with the neck part of your drumstick. In samba funk, performing the backbeat snare and bass

drum unison perfectly without any unnecessary flams is considered an art (Fig. 2).

D Section (Bars 25–40)
This is the keyboard solo where you have the opportunity to develop the part. The first part of the solo is notated, so follow this syncopated groove carefully.

E Section (Bars 41–53)
Following the eight bar drum solo, you return to the sign in section B. When repeating this section, do not play the written part again but feel free to develop it according to your musicality and understanding of the style.

Bar 41 | *Snares off*
This indicates that the snare will be played in the off position, where the snare wires do not touch the bottom drum head. This should be straightforward to do. However, not all snares have the same mechanism. Ensure that you know how to turn the snare wires off and on before starting the piece. The sound achieved when playing with the snares off is similar to the percussion instrument timbale. Using rim-shots, flams, drags and syncopated phrases will help you emulate the sound and feel with a great degree of authenticity. Turning the snare wires on can be done anywhere towards the end of the solo as long as you are ready to play when repeating section B.

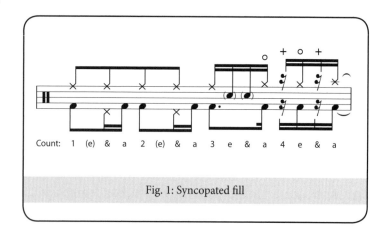

Count: 1 (e) & a 2 (e) & a 3 e & a 4 e & a

Fig. 1: Syncopated fill

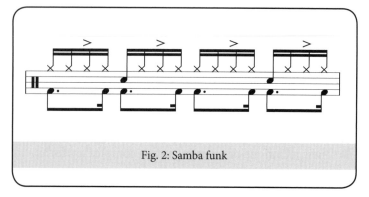

Fig. 2: Samba funk

SONG TITLE: SPACE FUTURE

GENRE: TRIP HOP

TEMPO: 90 BPM

TECH FEATURES: ADVANCED
CO-ORDINATION FILLS
6/8 TRIP HOP GROOVE
SNARE DRAGS

COMPOSER: NEEL DHORAJIWALA

PERSONNEL: NEEL D (PRODUCTION)
NOAM LEDERMAN (DRUMS)

OVERVIEW

'Space Future' is a trip hop track in the style of artists such as Massive Attack, Portishead and Tricky. It includes a 6/8 groove, advanced co-ordination fills and snare drags among its techniques.

STYLE FOCUS

In this track the metre changes from 6/8 to 4/4 while the tempo is maintained at the same value. This gives the impression of a tempo change which allows the piece to develop without losing its solid rhythmic drive. Indeed, it is this breakbeat style of groove, coupled with a heavy bass line, atmospherics and a lo-fi sound that gives this trip hop piece a sound that is typical of the genre. At the recording and mixing stages, the drums tend to be heavily compressed to make them sound more like samples.

THE BIGGER PICTURE

Trip hop is a downtempo, largely instrumental offshoot of hip hop that emerged in the early 1990s. Its exponents were inspired by hip hop's golden age of the late 1980s when hip hop producers developed the new technique of sampling into a complex art form.

The genre's birth can be attributed to the Bristol band Massive Attack whose 1991 album *Blue Lines* was an atmospheric, introspective riposte to hip hop and, especially, rap's block-rocking beats and cocksure vocal delivery. Tricky, the album's guest rapper, went on to release his own LP in 1995, the critically-acclaimed *Maxinquaye*. Geoff Barrow was the engineer at the studio where *Blues Lines* was recorded and, no doubt inspired by the sessions, formed the band Portishead, whose 1995 debut *Dummy* won that year's Mercury Prize. Tricky, Massive Attack and Portishead all hailed from Bristol and produced records similar enough to warrant the label trip hop, but they resented the term for fear of being pigeon-holed and pointed out that Tricky, although Bristol-born, was by this time resident in London. Regardless, by then trip hop was a global phenomenon with DJ Shadow in California and DJ Krush in Japan both recording for the Mo Wax label.

RECOMMENDED LISTENING

Massive Attack's 'best of' *Collected* gives an overview of their style but their debut record *Blue Lines*, 1994's *Protection* and 1998's *Mezzanine* are all excellent. *Dummy* by Portishead was inspired as much by spy film soundtracks as it was soul and funk 45s. Tricky's debut *Maxinquaye* is also recommended.

Space Future

Neel Dhorajiwala

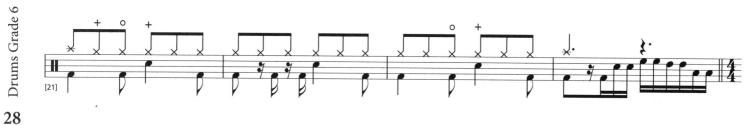

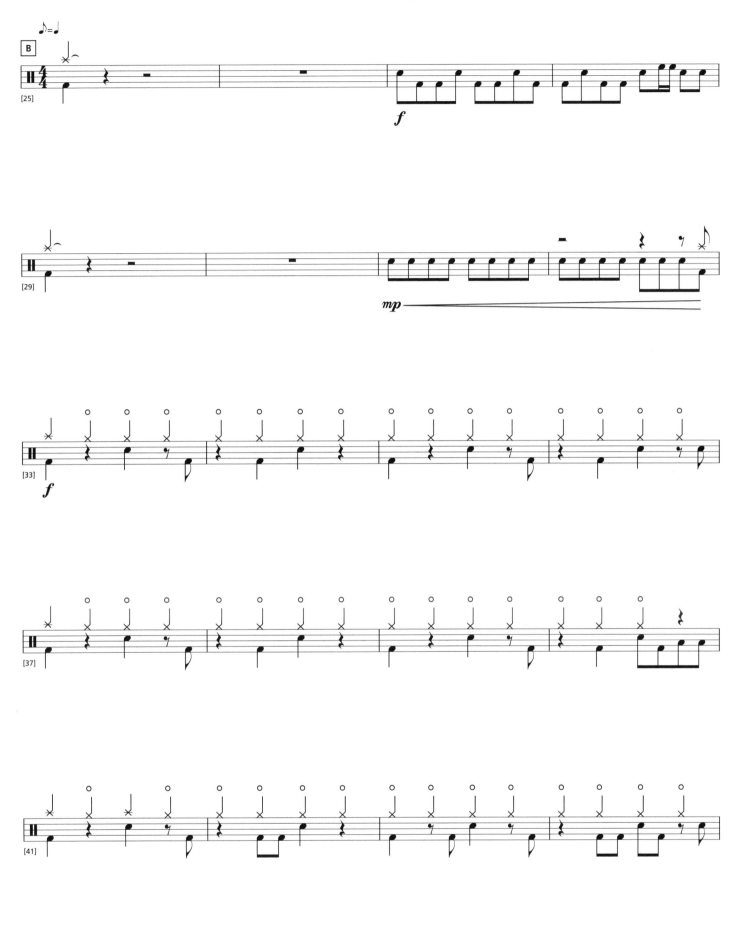

Drums Grade 6

29

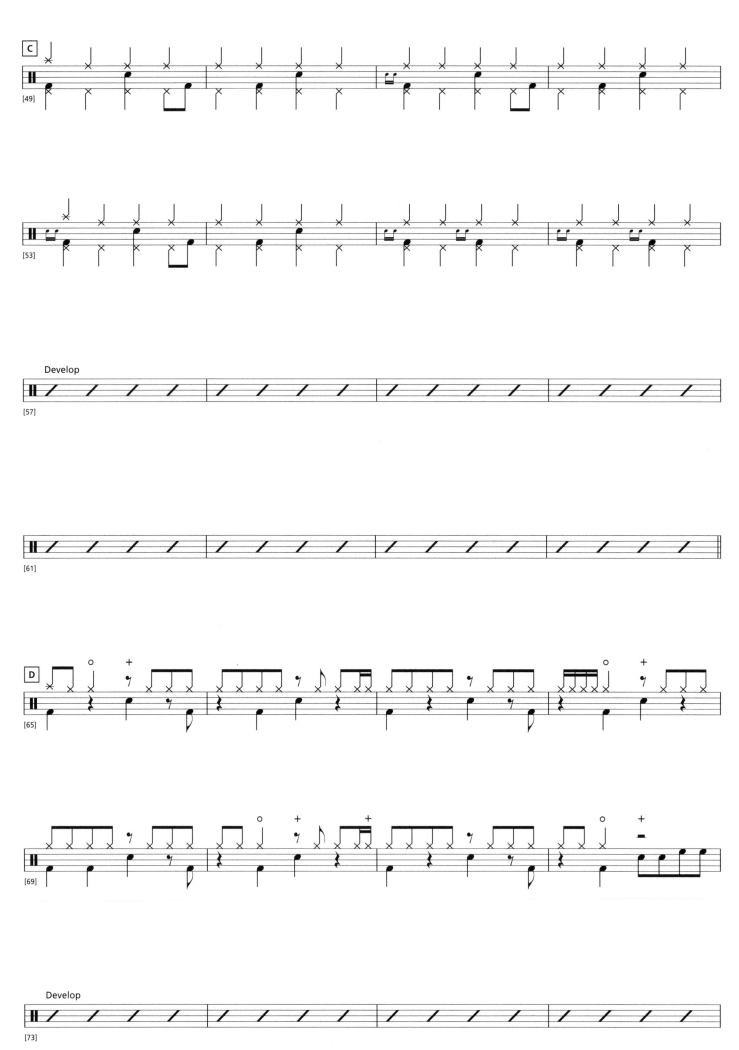

Walkthrough

A Section (Bars 1–24)
This section introduces a 6/8 trip hop groove. The consistent eighth notes are played on the ride and hi-hat, the cross stick on the fourth eighth note and the hectic bass drum pattern varies. The fill in bar 16 signals the entry of the snare in bar 17 where the groove intensifies.

Bar 1 | *6/8 trip hop beat*
This is a classic 6/8 trip hop beat where the eighth note leads on the ride cymbal are played with machine-like consistency. The cross-stick should be prominent in this groove, so make sure you hit the sweet spot of the rim and achieve a balanced projection. The 16th-note bass drums should be placed accurately between the eighth notes (Fig. 1).

Bar 24 | *Fill starting point*
Allow a 16th-note rest after the initial crash and bass drum stroke on beat one then begin the fill with the bass drum on the second 16th of the second eighth note. From there, continue with consistent 16th notes around the kit using alternate sticking until you reach the first beat of bar 25.

B Section (Bars 25–48)
Following the rhythmic change in bar 25, there are some written fills that build up towards the groove which is introduced in bar 33. This heavy open hi-hat groove includes offbeat bass drums and crashes.

Bars 25–26 | *Transition*
As notated in bar 25, there is a rhythmic transition and every eighth note will be equal to a quarter note. Ensure that you count the rests in these bars and internalise the new feel in order to enter with conviction in bar 27.

Bars 47–48 | *Fill across the bar*
In these bars the eighth notes are divided into groups of three, four, three and six eighth notes. This creates a challenging fill which you will play across the beats and even across the bar. Practise at a slower tempo and find the sticking option that allows you to move around the kit with ease. Ensure that these types of fills are played with fluency and a balanced sound. (Fig. 2).

C Section (Bars 49–64)
In this section the groove moves to the ride cymbal and there are drags on the snare and hi-hat foot on every beat. Grooves that demand four-way coordination can be challenging at first, but remember that in this specific groove the hi-hat foot pattern follows the ride cymbal.

Bar 51 | *Drag*
The drag rudiment consists of two grace notes followed by

one main stroke. In this groove, the drag is played on the snare and the main stroke on the bass drum and ride/crash. Make sure that you control the stick to achieve two even grace notes and time these well in between the quarter notes.

D Section (Bars 65–80)
The groove returns to the hi-hat, but the pattern is much busier with 16th-note phrases and open/closed sounds.

Bar 68 | *Drop pull*
These types of fast 16th notes are usually played with doubles. To achieve this you can use the drop pull technique. The basic concept is creating the second stroke in each group of doubles by pulling your fingers back and closing your grip.

E Section (Bars 81–84)
In this section, there is a four bar written drum solo which should be played as notated. The key to this solo is the sticking, so take your time and plan this in advance.

F Section (Bars 85–101)
The outro is the heaviest section in this piece with double crashes, open hi-hat and snare rim-shots.

Bar 85 | *Double crash*
Ideally, this will be played on two different crash cymbals. However, if you have only one crash cymbal in your set-up, use the ride cymbal as a crash but make sure you hit it with the neck part of your stick to produce the required sound.

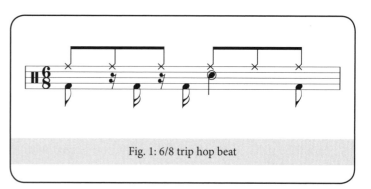

Fig. 1: 6/8 trip hop beat

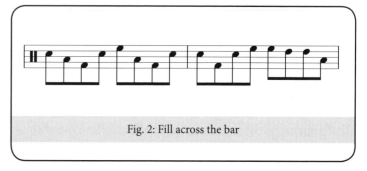

Fig. 2: Fill across the bar

You Can Call Miguel

SONG TITLE: YOU CAN CALL MIGUEL
GENRE: SOCA/CALYPSO
TEMPO: 116 BPM

TECH FEATURES: TRIPLET SHUFFLES
SYNCOPATED CADENCE

COMPOSER: KITA STEUER

PERSONNEL: STUART RYAN (GTR)
HENRY THOMAS (BASS)
NOAM LEDERMAN (DRUMS)
KISHON KHAN (KEYS)
FERGUS GERRAND (PERC)
RICHARD PARDY (SAX)
STEVE WALKER (TRUMPET)
ANDY CROMPTON (TROMB)

OVERVIEW

'You Can Call Miguel' is a soca- and calypso-inspired piece in the style of artists such as Harry Belafonte, The Mighty Sparrow and Arrow. It features triplet shuffles, a syncopated cadence and a dotted feel among its techniques.

STYLE FOCUS

Soca and calypso are both forms of dance music native to Trinidad and Tobago, so they have in common a driving beat. However, unlike disco, which emphasises every downbeat in a four-on-the-floor pattern, calypso and soca typically displace every other beat. The first and third accents are played with a dotted feel on the '1&' and '3&', which creates the rolling cadence in this song. You will often play with a percussionist or even a group of steel drummers when performing these styles of music so do not get too busy or you won't leave room for anyone else.

THE BIGGER PICTURE

Harry Belafonte put the rhythms of Trinidad and Tobago on the international music map in 1956 with his album *Calypso* which featured the breakthrough single 'The Banana Boat Song (Day-O)'. Traditional soca music features steel drums, but modern artists like Maximus Dan and Kevin Lyttle favour a more contemporary sound influenced by American R'n'B, with drum samples rather than live percussion or a blend of the two. The rhythms of soca and calypso have found their way into other musical styles. For example, David Garibaldi, drummer with the funk band Tower Of Power, has incorporated Caribbean rhythms into his grooves.

RECOMMENDED LISTENING

Harry Belafonte, the King Of Calypso, has recorded many classic, high energy calypso albums. *Jump Up Calypso* from 1961 features the irresistible track 'Jump In The Line'. The Mighty Sparrow has been recording calypso and soca albums since the 1960s and has won the title of Calypso Monarch 11 times. His lyrics are often politically charged but you can always dance to tracks like 'Jean and Dinah', 'Carnival Boycott' and 'Doh Back Back'. Arrow had his moment in the sun with 'Hot Hot Hot' but check out his 1992 album *Zombie Soca*. David Garibaldi's instructional DVD *Tower Of Groove* shows how he mixes soca into Latin and funk patterns on the track 'Soca/Rumba'.

You Can Call Miguel

Kita Steuer

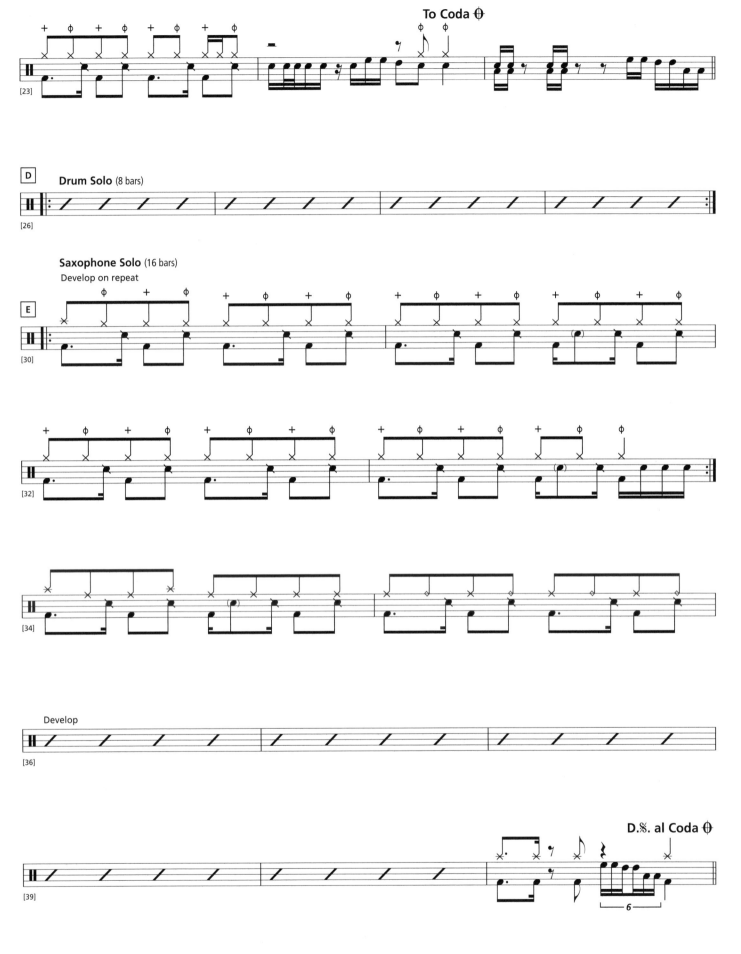

To Coda ⊕

D **Drum Solo** (8 bars)

Saxophone Solo (16 bars)
Develop on repeat

E

Develop

D.%. al Coda ⊕

⊕ **Coda**

Choke

Walkthrough

A Section (Bars 1–8)

This section introduces a calypso groove with cross-stick snare and bass drum on every beat as well as consistent eighth-note hi-hats. In bar 8 there is a stylistic fill that indicates the end of the section.

Bar 1 | *Calypso*

The cross-stick should be prominent in this groove. Aim to hit the sweet spot and maintain a consistent and balanced sound throughout. Focus on the unison between the cross-stick and bass drum, and avoid any unnecessary flams. Your right hand will move from the hi-hat to the floor tom on beat four for a three-part unison stroke.

Bar 2 | *Fingers technique*

In order to perform these fast 16th notes on the hi-hat with one hand, you will need to use the fingers technique. When using this technique, ensure that your thumb and index finger create a reliable fulcrum and utilise the other three fingers as a unit in order to manipulate the stick and perform fast multiple strokes. In this case, you need to play three strokes on the hi-hat with fluency and a balanced sound. Practise the hi-hat pattern on its own with a metronome for reference. Remember to pull your fingers back on the third stroke so that you are prepared for the next phrase (Fig. 1).

B Section (Bars 9–16)

The groove remains similar to section A but with a few added 16th notes on the hi-hat. In bar 16 the fill includes 32nd notes on the snare drum, so be prepared for this.

Bar 16 | *Thirty-second notes*

In this fill there are 32nd notes to perform. These are the next subdivision after 16th notes, so eight of them put together are equal to one quarter note. In order to understand the rhythm on beat one, start by playing the eighth note crash/bass drum hit followed by two 16th notes on the snare then double the 16th notes to create four 32nd notes. Try to play these with R R L L and use the drop pull technique. The basic concept of this is creating the second stroke in each group of doubles by pulling your fingers back and closing your grip. This should follow the first down stroke, where your fingers are loose after hitting the drum. Although this can be challenging at first, this technique will produce even doubles and can be used all around the kit in every style of music (Fig. 2).

C Section (Bars 17–25)

The classic soca beat is introduced in the chorus section with rim-shot snares, half open hi-hats and fills which are typical of this genre.

Bar 17 | *Soca*

The hi-hat pattern alternates between closed and half open, while the displaced snare on beats one and three gives this groove its unique feel. Secure co-ordination is the key here. Place the 16th-note snare exactly between the eighth-note hi-hats and keep your posture balanced while performing the complex hi-hat pattern.

D Section (Bars 26–29)

In this section there is an eight bar drum solo. Feel free to improvise according to your personal interpretation of the piece and style. However, remember that your synchronisation with the backing track must not be affected.

E Section (Bars 30–43)

The first 16 bars of this section are a saxophone solo. The initial groove develops on the ride in bar 34 and from bar 36 needs to be developed further. After the sextuplet fill in bar 41 you return to the sign in section B and play through until reaching the coda.

Bar 41 | *Sextuplet*

In order to perform this sextuplet well, you will need to have attained a reliable singles technique. As you are moving round the kit, the sticking R L R L R L is the most logical option. Focus on moving your wrists quickly and allow your arms to assist with positioning. Aim to hit all three toms in the middle of the drum head for maximum projection.

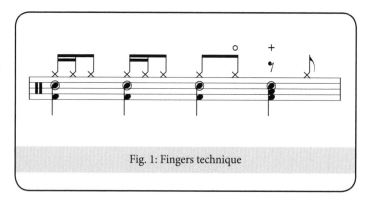

Fig. 1: Fingers technique

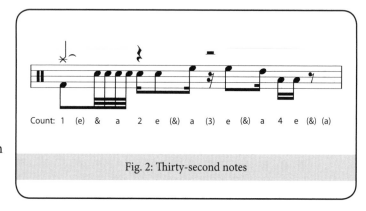

Fig. 2: Thirty-second notes

Technical Exercises

In this section the examiner will ask you to play a selection of exercises drawn from each of the five groups shown below. In Group E you will be asked to prepare *one* stylistic study from the three printed. The choice of stylistic study will determine the style of the Quick Study Piece. You do not need to memorise the exercises (and can use the book in the exam) but the examiner will be looking for the speed of your response.

The stickings shown (L & R) are there as a guide for right handed drummers. Left handed drummers should reverse the sticking patterns. **All exercises must be played to a metronome click.** Groups A–D should be played at ♩ = 80.

Group A: Single and Double Strokes
Single and double strokes in triplet eighth notes, 16th notes played alternately as a continuous exercise. To be played first time with singles and second with doubles

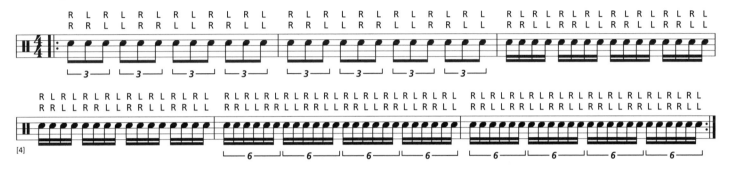

Group B: Paradiddles
Flam paradiddle in 16th notes and paradiddle-diddle in sextuplets

Group C: Ratamacues
Single ratamacue

Group D: Rolls
1. Five stroke roll phrase with accents on toms

2. Nine stroke roll phrase

Group E: Stylistic Studies

You will prepare a technical study from one group of styles from the list below. Your choice of style will determine the style of the Quick Study Piece.

1. Rock/Metal: half open hi-hat, busy 16th-note bass drum pattern

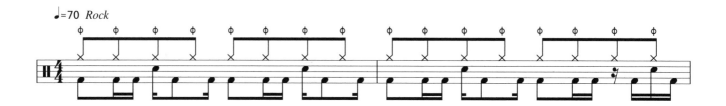

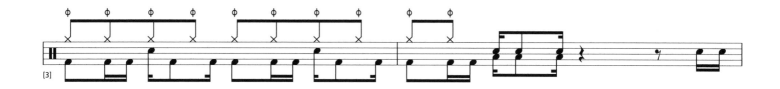

2. Funk: snare drum ghost notes, quick open/closed hi-hats

3. Jazz/Latin/Blues: polyrhythm, advanced co-ordination

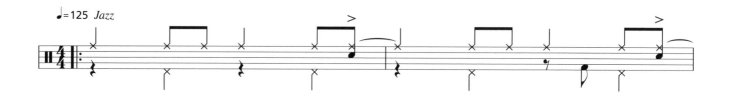

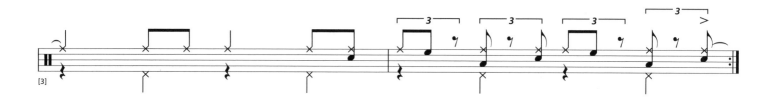

Quick Study Piece

At this grade you will be asked to prepare and play a short Quick Study Piece (QSP). Printed below are three examples of the type of QSP you are likely to receive in the exam. You will be shown the test and played the track with the ***notated parts played***. Any bars that require improvisation will not be demonstrated. You will then have three minutes to study the test. The backing track will be played twice more. You will be allowed to practise during the first playing of the backing track, with the notated parts now absent, before playing it to the examiner on the second playing of the backing track.

The style of your QSP is determined by the stylistic study you selected in the technical exercise section. The QSP is in the form of a lead sheet and it is up to you to create your own interpretation of the music in the parts marked for improvisation.

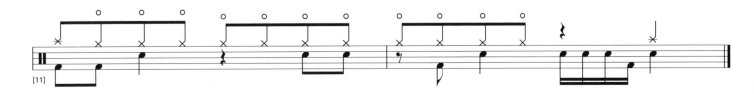

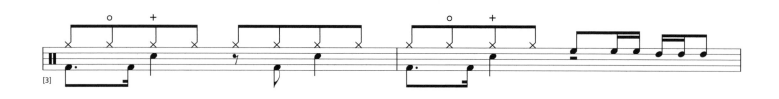

[3]

Develop

[5]

[7]

[9]

[11]

Ear Tests

There are two ear tests in this grade. The examiner will play each test to you twice. You will find one example of each type of test printed below.

Test 1: Fill Playback and Recognition

The examiner will play you a one bar fill in common time played on the snare drum. You will play back the fill on the snare drum. You will then identify the fill from three printed examples shown to you by the examiner. You will hear the test twice.

Each time the test is played it is preceded by a one bar count in. There will be a short gap for you to practise. Next you will hear the vocal count in and you will then play the fill to the click. The tempo is $\quarternote = 70$.

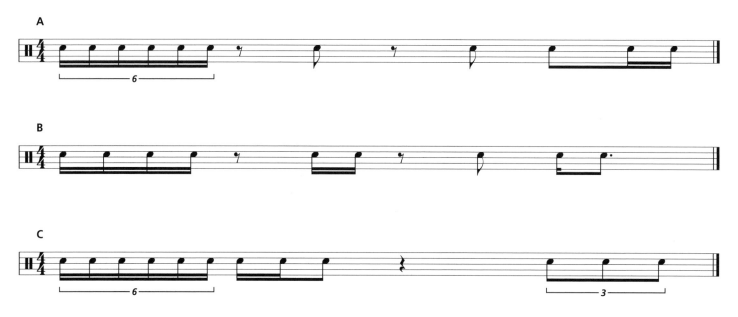

Test 2: Groove Recall

The examiner will play you a two-bar groove played on the whole kit. This is a two bar groove repeated. You will hear the test twice. You will be asked to play the groove back on the drum voices indicated for four bars then identify the style from four choices given to you by the examiner.

Each time the test is played it is preceded by a one bar vocal count-in. The tempo is $\quarternote = 80$–140.

A: Jazz
B: Metal
C: Samba
D: Funk

General Musicianship Questions

In this part of the exam you will be asked five questions. Four of these questions will be about general music knowledge and the fifth question will be asked about your instrument.

Music Knowledge

The examiner will ask you four music knowledge questions based on a piece of music that you have played in the exam. You will nominate the piece of music about which the questions will be asked. In this grade you will be asked to demonstrate your answers on your instrument as directed by the examiner.

In Grade 6 you will be asked to explain:

- Any notation used in the chosen piece

- Any dynamic marking found in the piece

- What makes the drum groove stylistically appropriate

- Use of drum voices, rhythms and techniques in drum solo sections

Instrument Knowledge

The examiner will also ask you one question regarding your instrument.

In Grade 6 you will be asked to explain and demonstrate:

- Care and maintenance of drums

- How to tune the drum kit according to the style of one of the pieces played

- How to produce: cross stick, choke cymbal, bell of ride, rim-shots, ghost notes, half open hi-hat, accents

Further Information

Tips on how to approach this part of this exam can be found in the *Syllabus Guide* for Drums, the Rockschool *Drums Companion Guide* and on the Rockschool website: *www.rockschool.co.uk.*

Entering Rockschool Exams

Entering a Rockschool exam is easy. You may enter either online at *www.rockschool.co.uk* or by downloading and filling in an exam entry form. Information on current exam fees can be obtained from Rockschool online or by calling +44 (0)845 460 4747.

- You should enter for your exam when you feel ready.

- You may enter for any one of the three examination periods shown below with their closing dates:

EXAMINATION PERIODS

PERIOD	DURATION	CLOSING DATE
Period A	1st February to 31st March	1st December
Period B	1st May to 31st July	1st April
Period C	23rd October to 15th December	1st October

These dates apply from 1st September 2012 until further notice

- The full Rockschool examination terms and conditions can be downloaded from our website. The information shown below is a summary.

- Please complete your entry with the information required. Fill in the type and level of exam and instrument, along with the examination period and year. Paper entry forms should be sent with a cheque or postal order (payable to Rockschool Ltd) to the address shown on the entry form. Entry forms sent by post will be acknowledged either by letter or email, while all entries made online will automatically be acknowledged by email.

- Applications received after the expiry of the closing date, whether made by post or online, may be accepted subject to the payment of a late fee.

- Rockschool will allocate your exam to a specific centre and you will receive notification of the exam showing a date, location and time, as well as advice on what to bring to the centre. We endeavour to give you four weeks notice ahead of your exam date.

- You should inform Rockschool of any cancellations or alterations to the schedule as soon as you can because it may not be possible to transfer entries from one centre, or one period, to another without the payment of an additional fee.

- Please bring your music book and CD to the exam. You may use photocopied music if this helps you avoid awkward page turns. The examiner will sign each book during each examination. Please note, you may be barred from taking an exam if you use someone else's music.

- You should aim to arrive for your exam 15 minutes before the time stated on the schedule. Guitarists and bass players should get ready to enter the exam room by taking their instrument from its case and tuning up. This will help with the smooth running of each exam day.

- Each Grade 6 exam is scheduled to last 30 minutes. You can use a small proportion of this time to set up and check the sound levels.

- You will receive a copy of the examiner's marksheet two to three weeks after the exam. If you have passed you will also receive a Rockschool certificate of achievement.

Drums Grade 6 Marking Schemes

ELEMENT	PASS	MERIT	DISTINCTION
Performance Piece 1	12–14 out of 20	15–17 out of 20	18+ out of 20
Performance Piece 2	12–14 out of 20	15–17 out of 20	18+ out of 20
Performance Piece 3	12–14 out of 20	15–17 out of 20	18+ out of 20
Technical Exercises	9–10 out of 15	11–12 out of 15	13+ out of 15
Quick Study Piece	6 out of 10	7–8 out of 10	9+ out of 10
Ear Tests	6 out of 10	7–8 out of 10	9+ out of 10
General Musicianship Questions	3 out of 5	4 out of 5	5 out of 5
TOTAL MARKS	60%+	74%+	90%+

PERFORMANCE CERTIFICATES | GRADES 1–8

ELEMENT	PASS	MERIT	DISTINCTION
Performance Piece 1	12–14 out of 20	15–17 out of 20	18+ out of 20
Performance Piece 2	12–14 out of 20	15–17 out of 20	18+ out of 20
Performance Piece 3	12–14 out of 20	15–17 out of 20	18+ out of 20
Performance Piece 4	12–14 out of 20	15–17 out of 20	18+ out of 20
Performance Piece 5	12–14 out of 20	15–17 out of 20	18+ out of 20
TOTAL MARKS	60%+	75%+	90%+

Drums Notation Explained

BASS DRUM & TOMS

Bass drum   Floor tom   Medium tom   High tom

SNARE

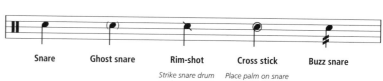

Snare   Ghost snare   Rim-shot   Cross stick   Buzz snare

Strike snare drum and surrounding rim at same time   *Place palm on snare drum head and strike rim with stick*

HI-HAT

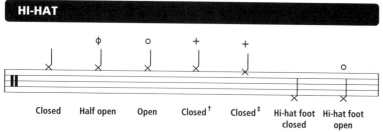

Closed   Half open   Open   Closed †   Closed ‡   Hi-hat foot closed   Hi-hat foot open

† *Used on the first closed hi-hat that follows an open hi-hat*

‡ *The hi-hat is closed without being struck. Note that the hi-hat closed (cross) symbol may appear above drum voices other than the hi-hat (as shown above). This simply means another drum voice is being played at the same moment that the hi-hat is being closed.*

OTHER CYMBALS

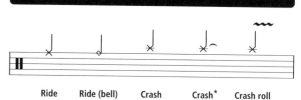

Ride   Ride (bell)   Crash   Crash*   Crash roll

Allow all cymbals to ring on *unless explicitly stopped, as indicated by the keyword* ***'Choke'***. *Occasionally ties may be used (*) to emphasise that cymbals should be allowed to ring on. This can avoid confusion during syncopations and pushes.*

GENERAL MUSIC NOTATION

Accentuate note (play it louder).

Slashes are used to demarcate bars during solos, fills, developments and other ad lib. sections.

D.%. al Coda

Go back to the sign (%) then play until the bar marked ***To Coda ⊕*** then skip to the section marked ⊕ ***Coda***.

Repeat the bars between the repeat signs.

D.C. al Fine

Go back to beginning of song and play until bar marked ***Fine*** (end).

When a repeated section has different endings, play the first ending only the first time and the second ending only the second time.

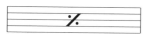

Repeat the previous bar. In higher grades these may also be marked *sim.* or *cont. sim.*

Repeat the previous two bars. In higher grades these may also be marked *sim.* or *cont. sim.*

In rudiments, each stem slash subdivides the note value by half.

MUSICAL TERMS WITH SPECIFIC EXAMINATION DEFINITIONS

Fill   Play an individual, stylistic fill.

Cont. sim.   Continue in similar way but vary the pattern slightly.

Develop   Extend the musical part in a stylistically appropriate manner.

Rit. (ritardando)   Gradually slow the tempo.

SONG TITLE: RAZORHEAD

GENRE: METAL

TEMPO: 168 BPM

TECH FEATURES: GHOSTING

BROKEN 16TH ROLLS

ODD TIME SIGNATURES

COMPOSER: JASON BOWLD

PERSONNEL: JASON BOWLD (ALL PARTS)

OVERVIEW

'Razorhead' is influenced by Slipknot, Sepultura and Bullet For My Valentine. You will find relentless, regular changes in rhythm and note values as well as dynamic subtleties and odd time signatures here.

STYLE FOCUS

Good technique and stamina are required to play metal convincingly. More importantly, an even consistency should be achieved with the volume of backbeats on the snare and the bass drum beats. This consistency should be continued into any drum fills so that the intensity level demanded by the style doesn't drop. Also, try to balance or mix yourself when playing metal because you may find that you tend to overhit the cymbals and hi-hats.

THE BIGGER PICTURE

The British band Black Sabbath are recognised as the creators of metal. Their self-titled debut was released in 1970, and soon after bands such as Judas Priest and Iron Maiden became part of the New Wave Of British Heavy Metal that influenced the faster sub-genres of thrash and speed metal in the 1980s.

Metallica, Anthrax, Slayer and Megadeth (also known as The Big Four) are the most famous of the bands that emerged from the 1980s thrash scene. The use of two bass drums became common practice among drummers Dave Lombardo (Slayer), Charlie Benante (Anthrax) and Lars Ulrich (Metallica), who were reaching speeds of 200 bpm.

In the 1990s nu metal bands Korn and Limp Bizkit mixed styles such as death metal and rap, while Slipknot continued to push the boundaries of speed thanks to their drummer Joey Jordison.

Since the turn of the millennium, the rise of groups like Lamb Of God, Mastodon and Trivium led to the New Wave Of American Heavy Metal, while the British group Bullet For My Valentine reached number 3 in the US Billboard charts in 2010 with their album *Fever*.

RECOMMENDED LISTENING

Jordison's drumming on *Iowa* (2001) by Slipknot is a great starter, as is Lombardo's work on Slayer's *Reign In Blood* (1986). For vintage drumming try Bill Ward on *Black Sabbath* and *Paranoid* (both 1970). For a modern approach, Ulrich's playing on *Master Of Puppets* (1986) features some excellent compositions.

Razorhead (Grade 7 Preview)

Jason Bowld

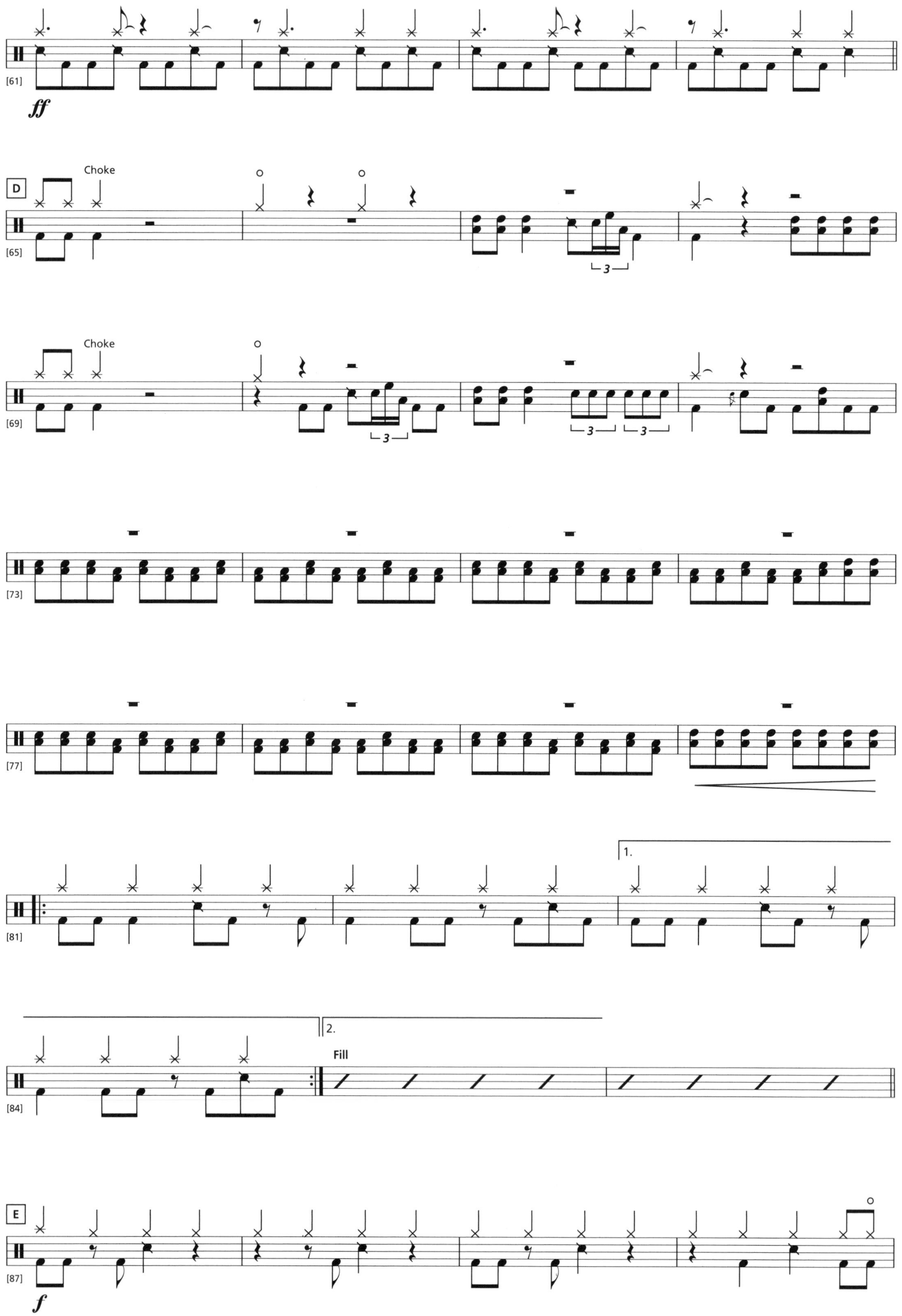
[61]
ff
D
Choke
[65]
Choke
[69]
3
[73]
[77]
1.
[81]
2.
Fill
[84]
E
[87]
f

Walkthrough (Grade 7 Preview)

A Section (Bars 1–16)
The intro is based on stabs which the drums solo around. This leads to the groove that locks in with the guitar riff.

Bars 1–8 | *Stab solo*
Try to emphasise the stabs throughout. They are counted as "1&2" and can be disguised within drum fills for added flow.

Bars 11–16 | *Groove fills*
In bar 12, the most comfortable sticking would be to use your left hand for the snare and travel around the crashes and toms with your right. Bar 16 concludes with a quarter-note triplet fill. Count "1-trip-let 3-tripl-let" to keep your timing accurate.

B Section (Bars 17–26)
This section can be interpreted as the verse of the song and features a heavy tom groove that accentuates the guitar riff.

Bars 17–25 | *Tom groove*
This groove is intense on the right hand so try not to choke the sticks, which will inhibit your speed.

Bar 26 | *Snare roll*
The key features of this roll are the offbeat accents before the beat. A loose grip is vital for power and consistency.

C Section (Bars 27–42)
This section features the chorus of the song and returns to the intro guitar riff but with a half-time feel.

Bars 27–34 | *Chorus groove*
The feel of this two bar groove is a mixture of normal and half-time. Focus on the crashes on beat one and beat three of each respective bar because these match the harmonic shifts in the music.

Bars 35–40 | *Half-time groove*
Watch out for the displaced backbeat onto beat four in the second bar of this two bar groove.

Coda (Bars 43–64)
The coda has a medium loud groove that increases dynamically towards the choruses.

Bars 43–52 | *Layered ghost groove*
After the coda's initial fill, you will play a groove in bar 45 which features a sticking that is similar to an inverted paradiddle: R L L R L R R L. The only difference is that the last right features a layered left double. There is a more fragmented approach and an open hi-hat on beat three of

the second bar. The pre-chorus snare roll returns in bar 52, where the dynamics increase to loud (Fig. 1).

Bars 53–64 | *Extended chorus groove*
Towards the end of this extended chorus, a two bar groove develops that must be played loud with snare and crashes on every dotted quarter note. The bass drum fills the gaps, so you will have to be careful not to rush your hands.

D Section (Bars 65–86)
This section features the three stabs that characterise the main riff of the whole song. These occur at the start of every other bar with the drums changing every eight bars, so use this as a compass to find your groove.

E Section (Bars 87–108)
This section starts with a drop in dynamics with a half-time groove that progresses to the 5/4 section.

Bars 103–105 | *5/4 groove*
Try counting "1&2 3&4 5&" as a way of tackling this groove's odd timing (Fig. 2).

F Section (Bars 109–119)
Make sure you observe that the final chorus should be played louder and faster than the others.

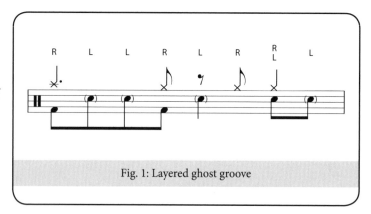

Fig. 1: Layered ghost groove

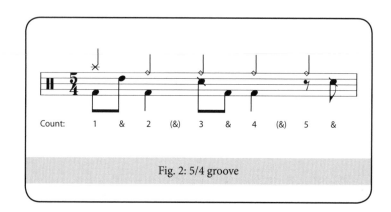

Fig. 2: 5/4 groove